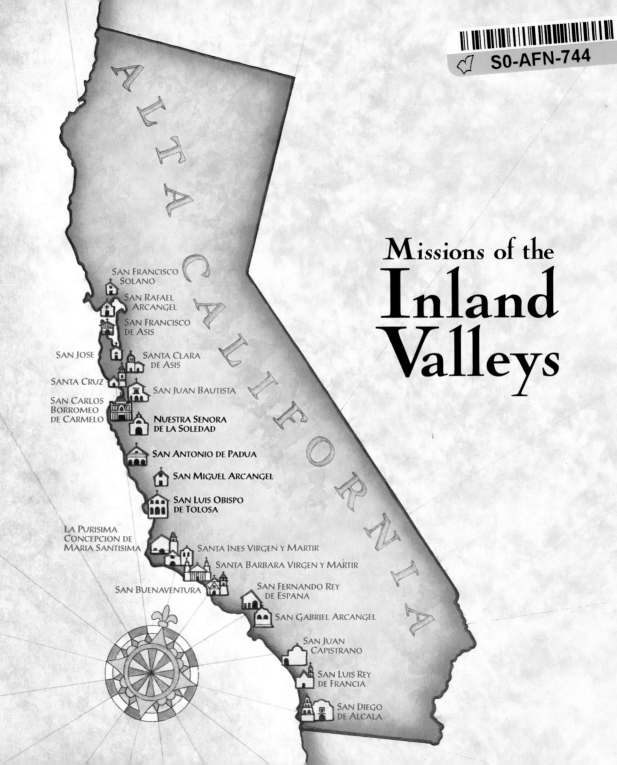

ALTA CALIFORNIA

San Francisco
Solano

San Rafael
Arcangel

San Francisco
de Asis

San Jose

Santa Clara
de Asis

Santa Cruz

San Juan Bautista

San Carlos
Borromeo
de Carmelo

Nuestra Senora
de la Soledad

San Antonio de Padua

San Miguel Arcangel

San Luis Obispo
de Tolosa

La Purisima
Concepcion de
Maria Santisima

Santa Ines Virgen y Martir

Santa Barbara Virgen y Martir

San Buenaventura

San Fernando Rey
de Espana

San Gabriel Arcangel

San Juan
Capistrano

San Luis Rey
de Francia

San Diego
de Alcala

# Missions of the
# Inland
# Valleys

California
MISSIONS

# Missions of the
# Inland
# Valleys

*Pauline Brower*

LERNER PUBLICATIONS COMPANY

Series editors: Karen Chernyaev, Mary M. Rodgers, Elizabeth Verdick
Series photo researcher: Amy Cox
Series designer: Zachary Marell

*This book is available in two editions:*
Library binding by Lerner Publications Company, a division of Lerner Publishing Group
Soft cover by First Avenue Editions, an imprint of Lerner Publishing Group
241 First Avenue North
Minneapolis, MN 55401 U.S.A.

Website address: www.lernerbooks.com

Library of Congress Cataloging-in-Publication Data

Brower, Pauline.
    Missions of the inland valleys / by Pauline Brower.
       p.  cm. — (California missions)
    Summary: Charts the histories of the California missions of San Antonio de Padua, San Luis Obispo de Tolosa, Nuestra Señora de la Soledad, and San Miguel Arcángel, and briefly describes the life of the inland valley Indian tribes, many of whom were Salinan, before the arrival of the Spaniards.
    ISBN: 0–8225–1929–1 (lib. bdg. : alk. paper)
    ISBN: 0–8225–9833–7 (pbk. : alk. paper)

    1. Spanish mission buildings—California—Juvenile literature. 2. California—History—To 1846—Juvenile literature. [1. Missions—California. 2. California—History. 3. Salinan Indians—Missions—California. 4. Chumash Indians—Missions—California. 5. Indians of North America—Missions—California.] I. Title II. Series.
F862.B82  1996
979.4—dc20
                                                                              95–2844

Manufactured in the United States of America
4 5 6 7 8 9  – JR – 08 07 06 05 04 03

*Cover: **Adobe walls— made of a clay soil—still stand at Mission San Miguel Arcángel.** Title page: Plants, such as cacti, that thrive in the dry climate of California's inland valleys decorate **Mission San Miguel's adobe wall.***

The author dedicates this book to five special Californios . . . Ben Jones, Mark, Paul, and Dan Keilbach, and Sam Early.

Every effort has been made to secure permission for the quoted material and for the photographs in this book.

# CONTENTS

# GLOSSARY

**adobe:** A type of clay soil found in Mexico and in dry parts of the United States. In Alta California, workers formed wet adobe into bricks that hardened in the sun.

**Alta California** (Upper California): An old Spanish name for the present-day state of California.

**Baja California** (Lower California): A strip of land off the northwestern coast of Mexico that lies between the Pacific Ocean and the Gulf of California. Part of Mexico, Baja California borders the U.S. state of California.

**Franciscan:** A member of the Order of Friars Minor, a Roman Catholic community founded in Italy by Saint Francis of Assisi in 1209. The Franciscans are dedicated to performing missionary work and acts of charity.

**mission:** A center where missionaries (religious teachers) work to spread their beliefs to other people and to teach a new way of life.

**missionary:** A person sent out by a religious group to spread its beliefs to other people.

**neophyte:** A Greek word meaning "newly converted" that refers to an Indian baptized into the Roman Catholic community.

**New Spain:** A large area once belonging to Spain that included what are now the southwestern United States and Mexico. After 1821, when New Spain had gained its independence from the Spanish Empire, the region became known as the Republic of Mexico.

**presidio:** A Spanish fort for housing soldiers. In Alta California, Spaniards built presidios to protect the missions and priests from possible attacks and to enforce order in the region. California's four main presidios were located at San Diego, Santa Barbara, Monterey, and San Francisco.

**quadrangle:** A four-sided enclosure surrounded by buildings.

**reservation:** Tracts of land set aside by the U.S. government to be used by Native Americans.

**secularization:** A series of laws enacted by the Mexican government in the 1830s. The rulings aimed to take mission land and buildings from Franciscan control and to place the churches in the hands of parish priests, who didn't perform missionary work. Much of the land was distributed to families and individuals.

# PRONUNCIATION GUIDE*

| | |
|---|---|
| Cabrillo, Juan Rodríguez | kah-BREE-yoh, WAHN roh-DREE-gays |
| Chumash | CHOO-mash |
| El Camino Reál | el kah-MEE-no ray-AHL |
| Esselen | EHS-suh-luhn |
| Ibáñez, Florencio | ee-BAHN-yehs, floh-REHN-see-oh |
| Lasuén, Fermín Francisco de | lah-soo-AYN, fair-MEEN frahn-SEES-koh day |
| Nuestra Señora de la Soledad | noo-EHS-trah sehn-YOH-rah day lah soh-lay-DAHD |
| Ohlone | oh-LOH-nee |
| Portolá, Gaspar de | por-toh-LAH, gahs-PAHR day |
| Salinan | suh-LEE-nuhn |
| San Antonio de Padua | SAHN ahn-TOH-nee-oh day PAH-d'wah |
| San Luis Obispo de Tolosa | SAHN loo-EES oh-BEES-poh day toh-LOH-sah |
| San Miguel Arcángel | SAHN mee-GAYL ahr-KAHN-hayl |
| Serra, Junípero | SEH-rrah, hoo-NEE-pay-roh |
| Vizcaíno, Sebastián | vees-kah-EE-no, say-bahs-tee-AHN |
| Yokuts | YOH-kuhts |

* Local pronunciations may differ.

# PREFACE

The religious beliefs and traditions of the Indians of California teach that the blessings of a rich land and a mild climate are gifts from the Creator. The Indians show their love and respect for the Creator—and for all of creation—by carefully managing the land for future generations and by living in harmony with the natural environment.

Over the course of many centuries, the Indians of California organized small, independent societies. Only in the hot, dry deserts of southeastern California did they farm the land to feed themselves. Elsewhere, the abundance of fish, deer, antelope, waterfowl, and wild seeds supplied all that the Indians needed for survival. The economies of these societies did not create huge surpluses of food. Instead the people produced only what they expected would meet their needs. Yet there is no record of famine during the long period when Indians in California managed the land.

These age-old beliefs and practices stood in sharp contrast to the policies of the Spaniards who began to settle areas of California in the late 1700s. Spain established religious missions along the coast to anchor its empire in California. At these missions, Spanish priests baptized thousands of Indians into the Roman Catholic religion. Instead of continuing to hunt and gather their food, the Indians were made to work on mission estates where farming supported the settlements. Pastures for mission livestock soon took over Indian land, and European farming activities depleted native plants. Illnesses that the Spaniards had unintentionally carried from Europe brought additional suffering to many Indian groups.

The Indians living in California numbered 340,000 in the late 1700s, but only 100,000 remained after roughly 70 years of Spanish missionization. Many of the Indians died from disease. Spanish soldiers killed other Indians during native revolts at the missions. Some entire Indian societies were wiped out.

Thousands of mission Indian descendants proudly continue to practice their native culture and to speak their native language. But what is most important to these survivors is that their people's history be understood by those who now call California home, as well as by others across the nation. Through this series of books, young readers will learn for the first time how the missions affected the Indians and their traditional societies.

Perhaps one of the key lessons to be learned from an honest and evenhanded account of California's missions is that the Indians had something important to teach the Spaniards and the people who came to the region later. Our ancestors and today's elders instill in us that we must respect and live in harmony with animals, plants, and one another. While this is an ancient wisdom, it seems especially relevant to our future survival.

*Professor Edward D. Castillo*
Cahuilla-Luiseño Mission Indian Descendant

# INTRODUCTION

FOUNDED BY SPAIN, THE CALIFORNIA **MISSIONS** ARE located on a narrow strip of California's Pacific coast. Some of the historic buildings sit near present-day Highway 101, which roughly follows what was once a roadway called El Camino Reál (the Royal Road), so named to honor the king of Spain. The trail linked a chain of 21 missions set up between 1769 and 1823.

Spain, along with leaders of the Roman Catholic Church, established missions and *presidios* (forts) throughout the Spanish Empire to strengthen its claim to the land. In the 1600s, Spain built mission settlements on the peninsula known as **Baja California,** as well as in other areas of **New Spain** (present-day Mexico).

The goal of the Spanish mission system in North America was to make Indians accept Spanish ways and become loyal subjects of the Spanish king. Priests functioning as **missionaries** (religious teachers) tried to convert the local Indian populations to Catholicism and to

*In the mid-1700s, Native Americans living in what is now California came into contact with Roman Catholic missionaries from Spain.*

teach them to dress and behave like Spaniards. Soldiers came to protect the missionaries and to make sure the Indians obeyed the priests.

During the late 1700s, Spain wanted to spread its authority northward from Baja California into the region known as **Alta California,** where Spain's settlement pattern would be repeated. The first group of Spanish soldiers and missionaries traveled to Alta California in 1769. The missionaries, priests of the **Franciscan** order, were led by Junípero Serra, the father-president of the mission system.

The soldiers and missionaries came into contact with communities of Native Americans, or Indians, that dotted the coastal and inland areas of Alta California. For thousands of years, the region had been home to many Native American groups that spoke a wide variety of languages. Using these Indians as unpaid laborers was vital to the success of the mission system. The mission economy was based on agriculture—a way of life unfamiliar to local Indians, who mostly hunted game and gathered wild plants for food.

Although some Indians willingly joined the missions, the Franciscans relied on various methods to convince or force other Native Americans to become part of the mission system. The priests sometimes lured Indians with gifts of glass beads and colored cloth or other items new to the Native Americans. Some Indians who lost their hunting and food-gathering grounds to mission farms and ranches joined the Spanish settlements to survive. In other cases, Spanish soldiers forcibly took villagers from their homes.

**Neophytes,** or Indians recruited into the missions, were expected to learn the Catholic faith and the skills for farming and building. Afterward—Spain reasoned—the Native Americans would be able to manage the property themselves, a process that officials figured would take 10 years. But a much different turn of events took place.

*Father Junípero Serra, a priest of the Franciscan religious order, dreamed of setting up missions in Alta California (modern-day California) and of teaching the Roman Catholic faith to the local Indians. He founded the region's first mission, San Diego de Alcalá, in 1769 and went on to establish eight more missions before his death in 1784.*

## Highlights of Present-Day California

- • City
- ⛪ Mission (see list below left)
- ▨ County
- —— El Camino Reál
- —— U.S. highway

### Miles
0 20 40 60 80 100

### Kilometers
0 40 80 120

### ⛪ CALIFORNIA MISSIONS

- A San Francisco Solano
- B San Rafael Arcángel
- C San Francisco de Asís
- D San José
- E Santa Clara de Asís
- F Santa Cruz
- G San Juan Bautista
- H San Carlos Borromeo
- I Soledad
- J San Antonio de Padua
- K San Miguel Arcángel
- L San Luis Obispo
- M La Purísima
- N Santa Inés
- O Santa Bárbara
- P San Buenaventura
- Q San Fernando Rey
- R San Gabriel Arcángel
- S San Juan Capistrano
- T San Luis Rey de Francia
- U San Diego de Alcalá

NEVADA

SIERRA NEVADA

CALIFORNIA

COAST RANGE

San Joaquin Valley

MOJAVE DESERT

PACIFIC OCEAN

Bodega Bay

Sonoma

San Pablo Bay

San Rafael
SAN FRANCISCO PRESIDIO

Alcatraz I.

San Francisco

Fremont

San Francisco Bay

San Jose

Santa Clara

Santa Cruz

Monterey Bay

MONTEREY PRESIDIO

Monterey
Carmel

Soledad

King City

San Miguel

San Luis Obispo

La Purísima

Lompoc

Solvang

Santa Ynez

Point Conception

Santa Barbara

SANTA BARBARA CHANNEL

VENTURA COUNTY

SANTA BARBARA PRESIDIO

Ventura

San Fernando

San Gabriel

Los Angeles

ORANGE COUNTY

San Juan Capistrano

Oceanside

San Diego

San Diego Bay

SAN DIEGO PRESIDIO

San Juan Bautista

Sacramento

Sacramento River

Stanislaus R.

San Joaquin River

Guadalupe R.

San Lorenzo R.

Pajaro R.

Salinas R.

Carmel R.

San Antonio R.

Nacimiento R.

Santa Ynez R.

Santa Clara R.

San Gabriel R.

Santa Ana R.

Los Angeles R.

Ventura R.

San Diego R.

Santa Monica Bay

SANTA BARBARA ISLANDS

San Miguel I.

Santa Rosa I.

Santa Cruz I.

Anacapa Is.

Santa Barbara I.

San Nicolas I.

Santa Catalina I.

San Clemente I.

UNITED STATES
MEXICO

MEXICO

BAJA CALIFORNIA

PACIFIC OCEAN

N

| California Mission | Founding Date |
|---|---|
| San Diego de Alcalá | *July 16, 1769* |
| San Carlos Borromeo de Carmelo | *June 3, 1770* |
| San Antonio de Padua | *July 14, 1771* |
| San Gabriel Arcángel | *September 8, 1771* |
| San Luis Obispo de Tolosa | *September 1, 1772* |
| San Francisco de Asís | *June 29, 1776* |
| San Juan Capistrano | *November 1, 1776* |
| Santa Clara de Asís | *January 12, 1777* |
| San Buenaventura | *March 31, 1782* |
| Santa Bárbara Virgen y Mártir | *December 4, 1786* |
| La Purísima Concepción de Maria Santísima | *December 8, 1787* |
| Santa Cruz | *August 28, 1791* |
| Nuestra Señora de la Soledad | *October 9, 1791* |
| San José | *June 11, 1797* |
| San Juan Bautista | *June 24, 1797* |
| San Miguel Arcángel | *July 25, 1797* |
| San Fernando Rey de España | *September 8, 1797* |
| San Luis Rey de Francia | *June 13, 1798* |
| Santa Inés Virgen y Mártir | *September 17, 1804* |
| San Rafael Arcángel | *December 14, 1817* |
| San Francisco Solano | *July 4, 1823* |

Forced to abandon their villages and to give up their age-old traditions, many Native Americans didn't adjust to mission life. In fact, most Indians died soon after entering the missions—mainly from European diseases that eventually killed thousands of Indians throughout California.

Because hundreds of Indian laborers worked at each mission, most of the settlements thrived. The missions produced grapes, olives, wheat, cattle hides, cloth, soap, candles, and other goods. In fact, the missions successfully introduced to Alta California a variety of crops and livestock that still benefit present-day Californians.

The missions became so productive that the Franciscans established a valuable trade network. Mission priests exchanged goods and provided nearby soldiers and settlers with provisions. The agricultural wealth of the missions angered many settlers and soldiers, who resented the priests for holding Alta California's most fertile land and the majority of the livestock and for controlling the Indian labor force.

This resentment grew stronger after 1821, when New Spain became the independent country of Mexico. Mexico claimed Alta California and began the **secularization** of the missions. The mission churches still offered religious services, but the Spanish Franciscans were to be replaced by secular priests. These priests weren't missionaries seeking to convert people.

By 1836 the neophytes were free to leave the missions, and the settlements quickly declined from the loss of workers. Few of the former neophytes found success away from the missions, however. Many continued as forced laborers on *ranchos* (ranches) or in nearby *pueblos* (towns), earning little or no pay.

In 1848 Mexico lost a war against the United States and ceded Alta California to the U.S. government. By that time, about half of Alta California's Indian population had died. Neophytes who had remained at the missions often had no village to which to return. They moved to pueblos or to inland areas. Meanwhile, the missions went into a state of decay, only to be rebuilt years later.

This book focuses on the four missions situated in inland valleys of the Coast Ranges, a chain of mountains that runs along the Pacific coast. San Antonio de Padua, established in 1771, was the first mission to be founded inland. San Luis Obispo de Tolosa (1772), Nuestra Señora de la Soledad (1791), and San Miguel Arcángel (1797) were also located in mountain valleys at least several miles from the coast. All four missions were built on land owned by Native Americans— the Salinan, the Northern Chumash, the Ohlone, and the Esselen.

*Series Editors*

*When the Franciscans opened a mission, a priest said mass for the Spanish soldiers and the Indian onlookers.*

# PART ONE

# Early Life along the Coast

THE ANCIENT HISTORY OF CALIFORNIA IS A STORY OF rock, water, and weather. On the slopes of the Coast Ranges, located near the Pacific shoreline, rain and melting snow fed rivers that flowed down the mountains through broad valleys before reaching the ocean. The rushing water carved lake beds and deep canyons along its path.

In these well-watered inland valleys, native grasses, wild berries, and other foods grew in abundance. Many different kinds of animals roamed the valleys and mountain slopes. Deer, elk, and antelope grazed on various shrubs and plants. Grizzly bears ate fish, berries, and nuts.

*Poppies are among the many wildflowers that cover California's mountain valleys every spring. Acorns from oak trees (inset) were an important food source for early Native Americans in California.*

17

Occasionally, the weather turned hot and dry for long periods. Without enough water from rain or melting snow, streams and rivers dried up, and large lakes turned into small ponds. Plants died during these droughts. Areas once covered in rich soil became desertlike.

## Native American Life

People disagree about where the native inhabitants of the inland valleys originally came from. Native American beliefs place native peoples in the region since the time of their creation. Others say that the ancestors of California Indians walked across a land bridge from Asia to Alaska and divided into smaller groups, some of which eventually moved southward. This land bridge, now covered by the waters of the Bering Strait, existed 20,000 to 30,000 years ago.

The Native Americans of the inland valleys were surrounded by beautiful willow trees that flourished beside sparkling streams. Large oaks grew on hillsides, dropping acorns that the people gathered for food.

The Salinan and Northern Chumash Indians eventually occupied most of the inland valleys of the Coast Ranges. Other inland valley tribes are the Ohlone and the Esselen. East of these four tribes lived the Yokuts Indians.

The Salinan and Northern Chumash usually stayed within their valleys. The looming

*Chumash pictographs (pictures painted on rock) can still be found in California.*

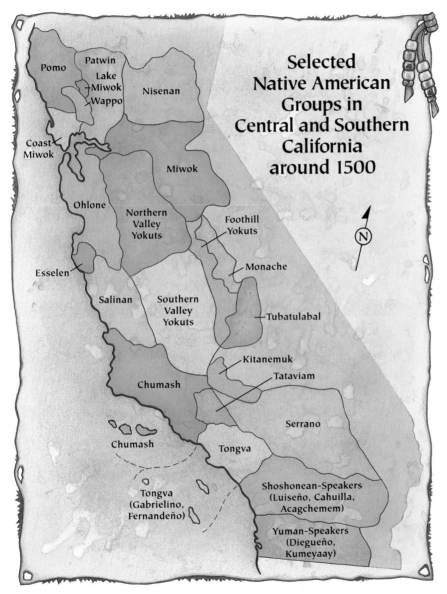

**Selected Native American Groups in Central and Southern California around 1500**

Pomo

Patwin

Lake Miwok

Wappo

Nisenan

Coast Miwok

Miwok

Ohlone

Northern Valley Yokuts

Foothill Yokuts

Esselen

Monache

Salinan

Southern Valley Yokuts

Tubatulabal

Kitanemuk

Tataviam

Chumash

Serrano

Chumash

Tongva

Tongva (Gabrielino, Fernandeño)

Shoshonean-Speakers (Luiseño, Cahuilla, Acagchemem)

Yuman-Speakers (Diegueño, Kumeyaay)

N

mountains surrounding these valley dwellers were difficult and dangerous to cross. The trees on the slopes grew close together, hiding deep canyons and fast-running streams. Mountain lions and coyotes lived in the highlands, and poisonous rattlesnakes and scorpions made nests among the rocks.

Inland valley Indians had little need to cross the mountains because the valleys almost always provided enough to eat. The men fished as well as hunted deer and small game for food. Women and children gathered seeds, pine nuts, and acorns. The Native Americans ground acorns into flour to make a variety of dishes, including porridge and cakes. When in season, wild strawberries, blackberries, and cactus fruits were also harvested.

The Native Americans crafted special tools to dig up large plants, whose roots were often prepared as food, medicine, or

19

cleansers. For example, the Indians pounded yucca roots against a boulder to make them soft and juicy for use as a soap and a shampoo.

The Indians of the inland valleys also took what nature provided to build dome-shaped houses. The Native Americans bent tree branches into frames and covered them with tule reeds. Many dwellings were large enough to house several families. Walls made of woven reeds divided the rooms.

Inland valley tribes sometimes crossed the mountains to trade with the Chumash who lived near the ocean. The inland valley people exchanged animal skins, nuts, and roots for seashells, which were carefully made into shell-bead money.

The valley tribes also fashioned shells into jewelry and tools. Using sea-lion whiskers, the Native Americans drilled small holes through thin shells and then strung them together

*Indians of the inland valleys constructed their dome-shaped homes from readily available materials such as reeds and tree branches. Designed to be built quickly, the dwellings enabled the Native Americans—who moved to different sections of their territories every season—to relocate with ease.*

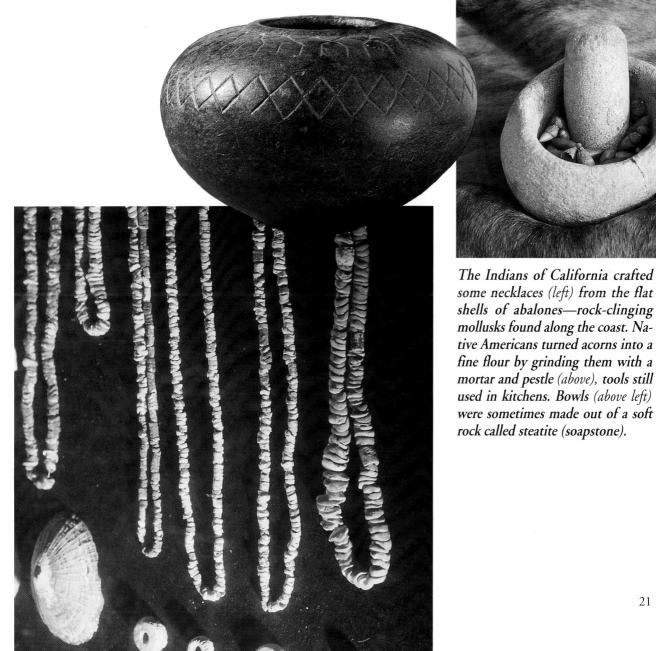

The Indians of California crafted some necklaces *(left)* from the flat shells of abalones—rock-clinging mollusks found along the coast. Native Americans turned acorns into a fine flour by grinding them with a mortar and pestle *(above)*, tools still used in kitchens. Bowls *(above left)* were sometimes made out of a soft rock called steatite (soapstone).

21

*Indian men gathered in temescals, or sweat lodges, to purify their bodies. A fire within the structure caused those inside to sweat heavily. Afterward they cooled off in a stream.*

to wear as necklaces. Large clam shells were used to scrape and clean animal hides.

The inland valley people built their villages near water sources such as lakes and rivers. Many villages lay along the Salinas, San Antonio, and Nacimiento rivers.

Waterways often formed the borders of a tribe's territory. Some groups made permanent marks on trees to show a boundary. Adults taught children where tribal borders were and to respect the territories of other tribes.

Each tribe's territory included hunting and fishing grounds. Crossing another tribe's boundary to fish, to hunt, or to take wild foods was forbidden. Tribal chiefs tried to settle territorial disputes through discussion. If that process didn't work, the tribes might go to war. But these wars did not last long. A chief usually stopped the fighting before too many people were hurt.

Chiefs were sometimes chosen for their wisdom and for their understanding of the environment and of people. A good chief also took advice from the villagers. Chiefs settled arguments among village families and knew the laws of the tribe.

Chiefs also acted as judges and determined punishments for tribe members accused of crimes. Thieves, for example, had to replace what was stolen. They also had to wear their hair hanging loose over their faces to show that they were in disgrace. Other villagers would have nothing to do with criminals. This system of government worked well for the people of the inland valleys.

Indians of the inland valleys practiced their own forms of religion and believed that everything on earth was part of a single spirit. Because they were also part of this spirit, the Native Americans respected their surroundings. They took from the wilderness only what they needed to survive and showed their gratefulness through prayer and public ceremonies.

Some older tribespeople were storytellers who passed on spiritual beliefs to the children of the villages. Storytellers also told of

# *The Eagle, the Sun, and the Moon*

The Indians of the Inland Valleys were great storytellers. One myth tells how Eagle created the earth:

*Many long years ago, before there were any people on the earth, the sea suddenly rose . . . and flooded the whole world [except for one mountain peak]. There on the summit gathered all the animals with Eagle as their chief. Then he said to Duck, "Cannot you dive down and bring some earth?" . . . At last [Duck] reached bottom and seized a little bit of mud. . . . Eagle took the earth that remained beneath [Duck's] nails [and threw it in four different directions]. Then the sea sank and the world became as it is.*

Another myth sees the sun and the moon as more than objects in the sky:

*Long ago, everything was able to converse, the sun, the moon, the stars and all the animals. Then the sun said, "These humans are great eaters; they eat all the time; I never see them sleep!" But the moon replied, "No, it is not so! They are great sleepers; they sleep all the time. When I look I never see them eating!"*

events that had happened to their tribes in the recent past. After the year 1542, some Native Americans in what is now California may have told their children and grandchildren about the arrival of white men.

## European Contact

In 1542 Juan Rodríguez Cabrillo, a Portuguese explorer working for Spain, landed his fleet on the Pacific coast of North America. The European sailors gave glass beads, cloth, and food to the Native Americans they met. Cabrillo kept journals and records of his trip to what became known as Alta California.

In 1603 the king of Spain sent another explorer, Sebastián Vizcaíno, to the shores of Alta California. Both Vizcaíno and Cabrillo drew maps and wrote descriptions of the coastline.

The explorers claimed Alta California for Spain, but more than 150 years passed before Spanish officials made any attempt to send settlers to the region. During the 1760s, King Carlos III of Spain learned that Russian and British ships were cruising the Pacific coast. He feared that these European rivals

*England had been interested in Alta California since the late 1500s, when the English pirate and explorer Sir Francis Drake anchored his ship, the* Golden Hind, *off the Pacific coast.*

*An illustration from the 1800s shows Franciscan priests baptizing an Indian baby to bring the child into the Roman Catholic community.*

convince the local Indians to be baptized. This religious ritual welcomed a person into the Catholic faith. The Spaniards referred to baptized Indians as neophytes.

Neophytes were expected to work without pay at the missions and to be loyal to the Spanish king. The missionaries planned to teach the neophytes to dress, work, and live as Spaniards did. Spanish officials determined that 10 years after being established, a mission would be turned over to its neophytes. In this way, Alta California would have an instant population of loyal Catholics who would strengthen the Spanish Empire's claim to the coastal region.

In July 1769, Portolá's expedition reached what is now San Diego. They began building Alta California's first mission—San Diego de Alcalá—and presidio. Soon afterward Portolá and a small group of men set off

would try to claim Alta California. Carlos decided to send land and sea expeditions to secure Spain's claim to the region.

In 1769 Father Junípero Serra and Captain Gaspar de Portolá led the first land expedition from New Spain north to Alta California. Portolá's job was to command the soldiers, to map the land, and to enforce the laws of Spain in Alta California.

Father Serra's job was to set up missions, where Franciscan *padres* (priests) of the Roman Catholic Church would try to

*In 1769 Captain Gaspar de Portolá led his expedition from New Spain to Alta California to help Father-President Junípero Serra establish the first missions in the chain.*

Gaspar de Portolá and his expedition endured many hardships, including near starvation, on their travels to find appropriate mission sites in Alta California. Riding horseback for days on end, the exhausted scouts were often unsuccessful hunters. According to Portolá, the weary group was sometimes forced to eat their pack mules "like hungry lions."

*Many elements, including easy access to fresh water, determined where the Spaniards located their missions. The Nacimiento River flowed near Mission San Miguel Arcángel and not far from Mission San Antonio de Padua.*

to find Monterey Bay, where the Franciscans would build a second mission and presidio.

Traveling along well-established Indian trails, Portolá's expedition soon reached the inland valleys of the Coast Ranges. That fall the group spent more than two weeks in the valleys, where they encountered several Salinan villages. Each village contained between 30 and 400 people.

The Native Americans—who had never before seen horses, guns, or men with light-colored skin—were curious about the Spaniards. Spanish clothing was unfamiliar to the Native Americans and so were beards, which very few Indians could grow. The explorers also spoke a language the Indians had never heard before.

On July 14, 1771, Padre Serra helped to place a cross in the valley of the San Antonio River, in Salinan territory. The cross was a symbol of the Christian religion the missionaries planned to preach to the Indians. Serra dedicated the site for the third mission in Alta California, which he named San Antonio de Padua, after Saint Anthony of Padua (a city in Italy).

# PART TWO

# Missions of the Inland Valleys

FATHER SERRA FOUNDED ALTA CALIFORNIA'S FIRST two missions on natural harbors—San Diego Bay in the south and Monterey Bay in the north. Knowing that New Spain delivered supplies to the settlements by ship, the Franciscans established most of the 21 missions near the shore. But because Father Serra wanted to reach as many Indians in Alta California as possible, he chose a valley of the Coast Ranges as the site of San Antonio de Padua.

*Behind the campanario (bell wall) at Mission San Antonio, neophytes built a barrel vault that led directly to the church.*

Although San Antonio faltered at first, the mission eventually grew into a prosperous spot famous for its water system, wheat, and horses. Another inland mission, San Luis Obispo de Tolosa, made a major contribution to mission architecture. The priests and neophytes at San Luis Obispo developed durable clay tiles, which in time replaced tule reeds as roofing material throughout the mission chain.

The other two inland valley missions, Nuestra Señora de la Soledad and San Miguel Arcángel, stood out in other ways. Mission Soledad, tucked away in an isolated mountain setting, had so few members and visitors that it became known as the Forgotten Mission. San Miguel, on the other hand, gained recognition for the colorful frescoes (paintings made on wet plaster) produced by the mission's artistic neophytes.

# Mission San Antonio de Padua

*Each mission kept track of its cattle by branding the animals with a symbol unique to the mission. The brand for San Antonio entwined the letters S and A.*

Mission San Antonio was first built near the San Antonio River about 75 miles south of the Presidio of Monterey. When settlers reached the site, they unloaded the pack mules that carried food and supplies, including a large bell for the new church. Father Serra directed some of his men to fasten the bell to a branch of an oak tree.

Soldiers and padres crafted a wooden cross and set it upright in the ground. After the cross was in place, Father Serra ran out to the bell and rang it enthusiastically. He yelled, "My heart . . . desires that this bell be heard all over the world." Serra wanted to convert all Indians to Christianity. He believed he was doing God's work.

While the Spaniards were building their first shelters at San Antonio, Father Serra noticed an onlooker. The father-president took gifts to the Salinan Indian and made friendly gestures in sign language. The Salinan left and came back later with other tribe members, who brought nuts and seeds to the Spaniards. Before long several Salinan were helping the padres build a wooden church and the priests' living quarters.

## A Rough Beginning

After founding San Antonio, Father Serra left to establish other missions. He assigned Padres Buenaventura Sitjar and Miguel Pieras to take charge of the new mission. Unlike most missionaries, these two priests began to learn the language of the Salinan Indians. Fathers Sitjar and Pieras realized that by knowing the language they'd be better able to teach Spanish ways to the Salinan. In turn, the Native Americans could explain their lifestyle to the Franciscans.

Padre Sitjar was pleased that the Salinan were helping him to build the mission. But he was

*Saint Anthony of Padua, the namesake for Mission San Antonio, was born in Lisbon, Portugal, in 1195. The Franciscan priest later moved to Italy, where he became a popular preacher, delivering sermons before large audiences.*

disappointed that the number of baptized Indians at the mission was so low. Two months after the founding, only 18 neophytes lived at San Antonio.

The Franciscans tried different ways to attract Native Americans to mission life. The priests offered the Indians gifts of glass beads, cloth, or food. Some Indians may have joined because they liked the beautiful robes the priests wore during church services. Bells and other religious items also impressed some Indians. If the padres could convince a chief to join, many of the villagers usually followed.

The padres at Mission San Antonio were eventually successful. In 1773 a friend of Father Serra, Father Francisco Palóu, wrote in his diary that Mission San Antonio "had baptized a hundred and fifty-eight Indians . . . fifteen neophyte girls had married neophytes, and three had married Leatherjackets [Spanish soldiers]. They were living very contentedly at the mission."

Mission rules stated that the neophytes should live at the mission soon after being baptized. They were allowed to return to their villages only for short visits. Any neophytes who failed to come back to the mission were considered to be runaways. The priests sent Spanish soldiers to look for runaways, who often faced harsh beatings upon their capture.

Baptized Indians joined the padres in the daily routine of work and prayer. Some neophytes seemed to enjoy their new life. Strict schedules and lack of freedom, however, caused many neophytes to run away.

Neophytes, who had never raised crops before, were taught to plow the land, to plant seeds, and to harvest crops. The neophytes also tended horses, sheep, and cattle.

The missionaries required many neophytes to learn a trade.

# Law and Order

A form of punishment common to Europeans in the 1700s was to flog, or whip, people who disobeyed. Franciscans also relied on this method of discipline in the missions. As a rule, floggings could include up to 25 lashes.

Neophytes were regularly punished for neglecting work or religious duties, for overstaying a visit to their village, for stealing, and for fighting. Non-mission Indians who hid runaways, stole mission livestock, or attacked a mission were sometimes flogged and sentenced to hard labor at a presidio.

*Spanish soldiers aim their guns at a neophyte who is trying to escape from a mission.*

*The Franciscans introduced many plants, including olive trees (left), to Alta California. Neophytes crafted candles (below) out of tallow, or the fat of butchered cattle and sheep.*

Men constructed buildings, made leather saddles and boots, cut stone, or fashioned iron goods. Some neophytes crafted furniture out of oak trees or chair seats out of leather cowhides. Indian women learned to make candles, soap, and cloth. The women also worked in the fields and pressed grapes for wine and olives for oil.

Mission San Antonio faced many problems during its first years. A drought in the early 1770s destroyed crops. In addition, the mission supply ship was stranded in New Spain while awaiting repair. San Antonio and other missions were left without food and other necessities.

Because of the drought, the San Antonio River dried up, and the priests and neophytes moved the mission a short distance to San Miguel Creek. At the new site, the missionaries and neophytes planted corn. It, too, was destroyed but this time by an early frost. Non-mission Salinan

33

Indians brought acorns and wild seeds to San Antonio, helping the settlement to survive.

## New Construction

Neophytes began the long process of making *adobe* (mud-brick) structures at the new site.

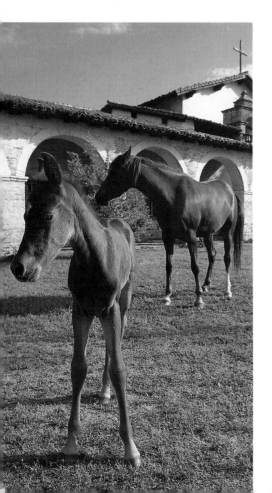

The mission buildings formed a **quadrangle,** which enclosed a central patio that was open to the sky. Storerooms, warehouses, shops, and sleeping quarters made up the buildings in the quadrangle. Neophytes also constructed a *monjerio,* or house for young, unmarried females.

San Antonio was the first mission to devise an elaborate water system. A dam on the San Antonio River forced river water into rock-lined ditches, called aqueducts, that led to the mission. When building the aqueducts, neophytes bonded the rocks together with mortar—a mixture of limestone dust, sand, and water.

*The horses (left) raised at Mission San Antonio had a reputation for being particularly hardy. Neophytes made adobe bricks (top right) by placing a mixture of clay, water, and straw into rectangular molds.*

The water system grew with the mission. Over the years, neophytes built miles of aqueducts to carry water to the mission's ever-expanding vineyards, orchards, and wheat fields. River water also turned the wheel of a gristmill, which ground wheat into flour for cooking. The aqueducts brought water to a bathing pool and to a fountain. As more Native Americans joined San Antonio, increasing the need for water, large reservoirs were created to store water for use during periods when the river ran low.

The water system at Mission San Antonio relied on a series of features. Channels called aqueducts carried river water to a reservoir *(bottom right)* for storage. Reservoir water was supplied on demand. When neophytes wanted to grind wheat at the gristmill *(right)*, for example, they released reservoir water into an aqueduct *(below)* that led to a water turbine beneath the mill. The water pressure forced the turbine to turn and the mill to operate.

In 1810 neophytes at Mission San Antonio began constructing a new, bigger church that had been designed by Father Pieras. They completed the adobe structure in 1813.

By this time, about 1,300 Indians were living at San Antonio. Herds of cattle and sheep numbered 17,000. The mission became famous for its hardy breed of horses. The mission's crops were abundant and its granaries full of wheat. The excellent water system helped the vineyard to produce huge harvests of grapes, which the neophytes made into a tart wine. Winemaking soon became an important business for San Antonio de Padua, which traded surplus goods to other missions for everyday necessities.

# Mission San Luis Obispo de Tolosa

*A stylish S shaped the hierro, or branding iron, at Mission San Luis Obispo de Tolosa.*

Portolá's 1769 expedition to Monterey Bay came upon a valley in the Coast Ranges that was dotted with holes. The Spaniards soon realized that the depressions had been made by grizzly bears digging for tule roots to eat. The soldiers, who were near starvation, shot a bear and ate its meat. Then they named the place La Cañada de los Osos (the Valley of the Bears).

The Spaniards shared their bear meat with a group of Northern Chumash, who often fished the nearby streams for their food. But if bears were close by the waterways, the Native Americans usually stayed away to avoid contact with the large and powerful grizzlies.

During the drought of the early 1770s, Pedro Fages—the governor of Alta California—remembered the Valley of the Bears. Fages, who had been one of the officers in Portolá's expedition, led a group of hunters to the valley. After three months, the hunters left with 9,000 pounds of bear meat to feed starving missionaries, neophytes, and soldiers. In exchange for some of the meat, the Northern Chumash gave loads of edible seeds to Fages's group.

## A New Mission Site

Meanwhile, Padre Serra had decided that the Northern Chumash territory would make a good site for the fifth Franciscan mission in Alta California. On September 1, 1772, Spanish soldiers planted a cross for Mission San Luis Obispo de Tolosa, named for Saint Louis,

*A statue of a bear outside the church at Mission San Luis Obispo honors the many grizzlies that once roamed the area.*

the bishop of Toulouse (a city in France). The mission was situated on a hill about 15 miles inland from the Pacific Ocean and overlooked the Valley of the Bears. The soldiers thought Mission San Luis Obispo could provide shelter for bear hunters and other passersby.

After dedicating the new mission, Padre Serra left Padre José Cavaller, two neophytes, and five soldiers to begin building the mission community. Padre Cavaller had a small amount of brown sugar and beads to trade with the Northern Chumash for seeds and other food. The priest also had flour as well as corn and bean seeds.

Some Chumash came to the site to help the Spaniards build the mission. They gave the priest food but did not want any Spanish gifts. A few Indians brought their children to the church for baptism. Later more adult Native Americans joined the mission. But most Chumash were not eager to become neophytes. The poverty-stricken mission was unappealing. The Native Americans had no good reason to abandon their lifestyle.

Mission life at San Luis Obispo—as at other missions—had many other disadvantages.

> THE POVERTY-STRICKEN MISSION WAS UNAPPEALING. THE NATIVE AMERICANS HAD NO GOOD REASON TO ABANDON THEIR LIFESTYLE.

Neophytes often faced harsh punishment for not following the rules of the missionaries. Priests sometimes ordered the mission soldiers to whip or beat neophytes for offenses large and small. After being baptized, Indians were supposed to stop practicing their own religious rituals and had to labor for long hours in mission fields and workshops without pay.

## Up in Smoke

Before long, neophyte laborers at Mission San Luis Obispo produced a variety of harvests that were better than expected. The mission, which also occupied good hunting grounds, began to attract more Indians.

But a tribe of Indians who lived farther inland—enemies of the neophytes at San Luis Obispo—attacked the mission. The raiders shot flaming arrows into the tule-reed roofs of the mission, burning down all but two of the buildings. Spanish soldiers caught two of the Native Americans and sent them to the Presidio of Monterey for punishment. But other raids followed.

Father Cavaller worked on rebuilding the mission. He showed the neophytes how to make adobe bricks for the walls of the new buildings. The adobe kept rooms cool in the summer and warm in the winter.

Because of the attacks, Padre Cavaller designed fireproof roof tiles, called *tejas,* that were modeled after roof tiles used in Spain. The neophytes shaped the tiles out of strips of wet clay, which were placed over a smooth tree limb to dry into rounded shapes. To strengthen the dried tiles, the neophytes baked them in an oven. The tiles protected the buildings from burning arrows and from rain, which could ruin adobe. Because the tiles proved to be so successful, all the other missions were manufacturing them before long.

*Fireproof tiles, first used in Alta California at Mission San Luis Obispo, eventually covered the roofs of all 21 missions in the chain.*

*Neophytes were responsible for plowing acres of mission property.*

In 1798 Padre Luís Antonio Martínez joined San Luis Obispo and made many improvements. He introduced the mission to the growing of different fruits and to the making of olive oil. As time passed, the mission began raising cattle at two nearby ranchos it had established.

Mission San Luis Obispo soon became a successful business. The mission ranchos eventually sold tallow (cattle fat used to make candles and soap) to foreign merchants. These traders also bought cattle hides—which were fashioned into shoes, saddles, and other leather products—and shipped them to Europe and the United States.

# Mission Nuestra Señora de la Soledad

Vaqueros, *or cowboys who had learned the trade of branding cattle, burned this mark onto the calves at Mission Nuestra Señora de la Soledad.*

During the 1769 land expedition to find Monterey Bay, Portolá's scouts thought at one point that they had come upon the large body of water. Padre Juan Crespí kept a detailed journal during this expedition. His diary says that the men believed "the goal toward which [they] were marching was only a short distance away."

Disappointment came when the explorers realized they were seeing a mirage—a false image produced by heat waves. In reality the tired men were looking over a wide, flat valley in the Coast Ranges. The mysterious Monterey Bay was yet to be found. The mirage, however, would become the site of Alta California's thirteenth mission.

Portolá and his men made their camp in the valley, which lay in Salinan territory south of the Presidio of Monterey and several miles inland from the Pacific Ocean. A small group of Salinan soon approached the explorers. One of the Indians uttered a word that resembled *soledad,* the Spanish term for "solitude." Padre Crespí made a note of it in his diary.

At the time, Portolá figured that the valley was a good place to build a mission. The site lay halfway between San Antonio and Monterey. Travelers would welcome a stopping point between these two settlements. In addition, the Native Americans in the area were friendly, and the Salinas River flowed nearby. But Portolá did not yet know that summers in the valley were hot and winters damp and cold. Nor did he know that the area was home to only a small population of Native Americans.

*The weary members of Portolá's 1769 expedition mistook the valley that now holds Mission Soledad to be a large body of water.*

On October 9, 1791, Padre Fermín Francisco de Lasuén, who became father-president after Padre Serra died in 1784, blessed the valley as the site of the thirteenth mission. Remembering Padre Crespí's diary, the priests named the mission Nuestra Señora de la Soledad (Our Lady of Solitude) for Mary, the mother of Jesus.

## A Troubled Mission

From its founding, Soledad was a troubled and lonely mission. The money New Spain sent to help start the mission got lost. Other missions sent gifts, but the priests needed more than they received.

The area's damp weather caused several padres to become ill after only a few months at Soledad. Dozens of missionaries were stationed at Soledad over the years. At least 30 of them asked to be moved to another mission. With so many padres leaving, the task of persuading Native Americans to join the mission grew more difficult.

The spread of disease added to the mission's problems. A mysterious deadly disease swept through the community in 1802, killing several neophytes a day. Many neophytes, worried that they would catch the sickness, ran away.

At Soledad as well as at the other missions in Alta California, disease was the number-one

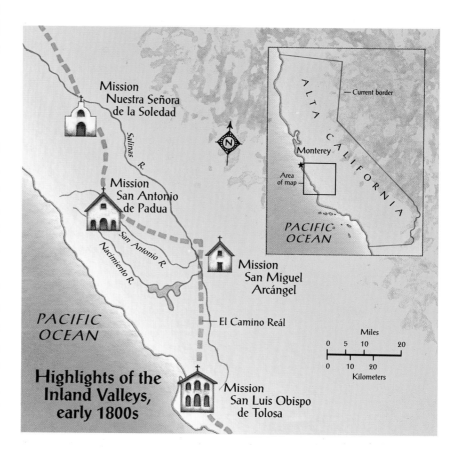

Highlights of the Inland Valleys, early 1800s

*Smallpox, a leading cause of death among neophytes, began with a high fever before causing a rash of small pimples to cover the body.*

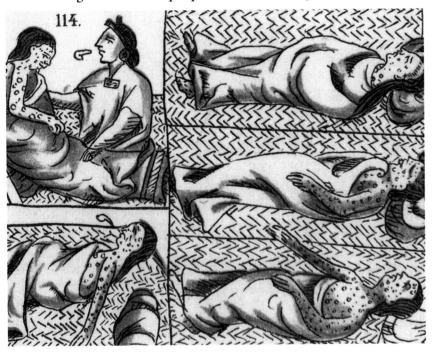

Compared to other missions, Nuestra Señora de la Soledad had few neophytes. Its small labor force took more than six years to replace the mission's temporary, thatched shelters with adobe buildings.

killer of neophytes. The Spaniards unintentionally exposed the Indians to European diseases such as smallpox and influenza. Because the native peoples had never before come into contact with these illnesses, their bodies had not developed a natural resistance. Thousands of Indians died shortly after joining the missions.

Mission Soledad also suffered a series of natural disasters. The Salinas River flooded three times in eight years, each time destroying part of the mission. Earthquakes occasionally shook and weakened the buildings. In addition, the climate in the region caused the adobe to dry out in the heat and to swell when it rained.

## The Forgotten Mission

Padre Florencio Ibáñez was stationed at Mission Soledad in 1803. He was determined to

baptize more Indians, grow more crops, and raise more animals. Two years after the priest arrived, the mission reached its highest number of neophytes— 688.

Father Ibáñez believed in organization and hard work. He set up a strict schedule at the mission. The bells rang at sunrise, when the priest and neophytes went to the church together for prayers and religious instruction. Padre Ibáñez felt that teaching the Catholic faith to the neophytes was the most important part of his work.

When the bell rang a second time, breakfast was served. The neophyte women who prepared the meal had started working before sunrise. A third bell signaled work time. Some men and boys went to the fields to plant, cultivate, or harvest crops. Others made boots and saddles in the leather shop. Women labored at the looms making cloth or in the kitchen preparing *atole* (porridge with pieces of meat). The noon bell announced lunchtime, when the Franciscans and neophytes ate their biggest meal of the day.

Padre Ibáñez could often be found in his room, where he carefully recorded the number of crops produced, the animals born at the mission, and the number of baptisms performed. He also made plans for the following days.

In the evenings, the neophytes sometimes sang and played musical instruments. The neophytes also performed in plays written by the padre. The entertainment helped the Indians to relax and enjoy themselves after a hard day's work.

Father Ibáñez managed the mission well. During his 15 years at Soledad, the herds of cattle and sheep continually grew larger. The neophytes tanned cattle hides to make leather for trade. Food production increased. Yet Mission Soledad was never as successful as many of the other missions. Few Indians lived near Soledad, and the population of the isolated community grew slowly. In addition, the mission rarely had visitors. Some people called Soledad the Forgotten Mission.

On one occasion, however, Mission Soledad did receive a large number of visitors. In November 1818, a pirate named Hippolyte de Bouchard sailed two black ships into Monterey Bay. The pirates fired their cannon at the presidio and then went ashore with guns. They invaded Monterey, the capital of Alta California, destroying what they could and stealing what they wanted.

*To help teach the neophytes how to read music, the Franciscans copied musical notations in two colors.*

Padres, soldiers, and the governor of Alta California fled inland seeking shelter. Soledad, three miles from El Camino Reál, became a place of safety for the people of Monterey. The mission had never had so many guests.

A few days later, after learning the pirates were gone, the visitors prepared to return to the coast. Before leaving, Vicente Sarría— the father-president at the time—buried Padre Ibáñez, who had died meanwhile of natural causes.

# Mission San Miguel Arcángel

In the summer of 1797, Father-President Lasuén founded five missions in Alta California. Three of them were in the north, one in the south, and one in an inland valley, two days' ride south of Soledad. The inland valley mission was San Miguel Arcángel, named after Saint Michael, an archangel (chief angel) and a guardian of Israel.

*Oak trees (top) dot a hillside near San Miguel Arcángel. The mission's branding iron (left) looked like the number three.*

The land Padre Lasuén selected for the mission seemed perfect. The Salinas and Nacimiento Rivers joined nearby, providing enough water for crops. A large group of Salinan Indians lived close to the site. The padres believed this was a good sign. They made plans to baptize Native Americans and to build a new community.

Many Salinan watched the founding ceremonies on July 25. The religious service started with the loud ringing of bells on the brushwood altar, where a statue of the Virgin Mary stood. One padre sprinkled holy water on a large cross the soldiers had made. Then the padre blessed the surrounding ground and named the mission.

## The Right Religion

The padres baptized 15 Native American children that day. Padre Lasuén wrote in his journal, "These ceremonies were conducted . . . in the presence of a great multitude of pagans [people who worship more than one god] of both sexes and all ages, whose pleasure and rejoic-

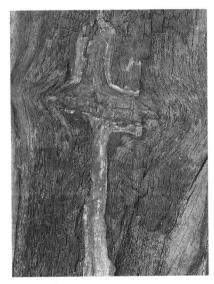

*A cross carved on an oak tree near Mission San Miguel signaled to travelers that they were still on El Camino Reál, or the mission trail.*

ing exceeds our expectations, thanks be to God."

When the ceremonies were over, the Indians helped the padres and soldiers to construct a wooden shelter. Padre Lasuén soon left for another mission site. Eventually, he assigned Padres Juan Martín and Juan Cabot to manage San Miguel.

The priests at San Miguel and at other missions were devout Catholics eager to share their spiritual faith with Native Americans. The Franciscans believed strongly that Catholicism was the only true religion. The missionaries felt that Native American religions worshiped false gods. For this reason, most missionaries forbade neophytes from performing Native American religious ceremonies and rituals.

Many neophytes, however, held fast to their spiritual beliefs, practicing religious ceremonies and rituals in secret. For these Native Americans, attending Catholic mass and reciting prayers in Spanish and in Latin (the language of the Church) were done to avoid punishment.

# Troubled Padre

Padres Buenaventura Sitjar and Antonio de la Concepcion Horra were the first priests to be stationed at San Miguel Arcángel. Father Horra's service, however, lasted only two months. Alarmed by Father Sitjar's methods, Father Horra charged his partner with mismanagement of the grounds and with abuse of the neophytes. Within weeks the Church, claiming that Father Horra had gone insane, sent him back to New Spain.

In New Spain, Father Horra wrote a letter to his superiors accusing the missionaries in Alta California of many wrongdoings. These included not requiring the neophytes to learn Spanish, allowing baptized Indians to live in their villages, not providing enough food for laborers, and punishing neophytes excessively.

"The treatment shown to the Indians," wrote Father Horra, "is the most cruel I have ever read in history. For the slightest things they receive heavy floggings, are shackled, and put in the stocks, and treated with so much cruelty that they are kept whole days without a drink of water."

Authorities soon conducted an investigation, requiring the priests to answer a 15-question survey. Although the results of the survey indicated that Father Horra's accusations were probably real and not a result of insanity, the Church declared Father Horra's charges to be unfounded. Many historians, however, consider his letter and the results of the survey to be rare and reliable sources of information about daily life at the missions.

Regardless of religious beliefs at San Miguel, the mission continued to grow. Neophytes built a quadrangle, and the mission quickly became a thriving community. By the end of San Miguel's first year, 185 neophytes were working at the mission.

The first crops at San Miguel were successful. Barley, corn, peas, and beans grew well in the fertile soil. The mission granaries held hundreds of bushels of wheat. The mission needed little outside help or supplies.

*A paw print (left), set before the tile was completely dry, can still be seen on the floor of Mission San Miguel. The arches (above) along San Miguel's colonnade are of various heights and widths, a feature unique to that mission.*

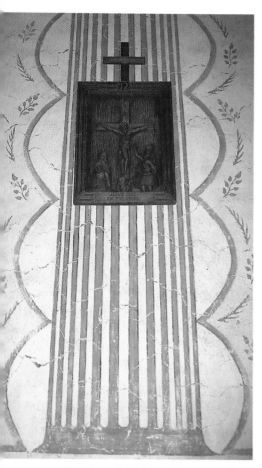

*The frescoes (above, facing page), or murals painted on wet plaster, produced by Estéban Munras and the neophytes at San Miguel are still in excellent condition, making the mission church one of the most colorful in the chain.*

The building of Mission San Miguel continued for years. Thick adobe walls and tile roofs replaced most of the first wooden shelters. Some buildings had floor tiles. As the community grew larger, neophytes constructed more houses, storage buildings, and workrooms. After eight years, 949 neophytes were living at San Miguel.

In 1806 tragedy struck the mission. A fire raged through the community, destroying buildings and supplies. In addition to wool and cloth, 6,000 bushels of wheat were lost in the flames.

## Church Art

After the fire destroyed the mission church, the priests at San Miguel began planning a new, larger adobe church. When neophytes finished building it in 1818, Padre Cabot sent for his friend Estéban Munras, a well-known Spanish artist. Munras had worked with neophytes at other mission churches. He agreed to teach the neophytes at San Miguel how to plaster and how to fresco (to paint on wet plaster) the inside of the new church.

Munras studied the mission and made sketches detailing the designs to be painted on the plaster. He got his ideas by looking at illustrations found in the mission's library books. When the drawings were complete, the Indians mixed fresh plaster. They used ground cobalt and other minerals to make red, brown, orange, yellow, and greenish blue paints. Munras added cactus juice to the colors to make them last.

Neophytes watched as Munras spread fresh plaster across a section of wall. He then traced his drawings on the wet plaster and quickly applied the bright colors. The paint would become part of the plaster, so the work had to be finished before the plaster dried. Soon the neo-

phytes were creating their own frescoes.

Visitors to San Miguel enjoyed the beautiful fresco paintings. The artwork impressed a traveler from the eastern United States named Alfred Robinson. He made notes in his journal about the frescoes and how well he thought the padres managed the mission. He also described the hot summer weather: "The fleas cannot endure the summer months, and during the heat of the day may be seen gasping upon the brick pavements!"

The mission grew into a huge estate. By the early 1800s, the northern and southern boundaries of San Miguel lay 50 miles apart. Almost 2,000 neophytes were living at the mission. They worked the fields and tended about 10,000 head of cattle and 1,500 horses, as well as large herds of sheep, pigs, and goats and a pack of mules. The fertile fields yielded large harvests of grains, fruits, and vegetables.

# PART THREE

# Secularization of the Missions

IN 1810 THE PEOPLE OF NEW SPAIN REBELLED AGAINST unfair laws and high taxes imposed by their Spanish rulers. In 1821, after 11 years of war, the people of New Spain won their independence and formed the Republic of Mexico. Alta California became part of this new country.

For many people living in Alta California, raising the Mexican flag was difficult to accept. The priests were still loyal to Spain.

*In this early-nineteenth-century drawing of Mission San Antonio, two wooden figureheads sit atop the gateway. Sailors who were grateful for having survived a stormy journey by sea supposedly gave the pieces to the mission.*

Many of the retired Spanish soldiers, who had developed large ranchos, worried that the new government would seize their land and livestock.

The Mexican government soon revealed its plans for Alta California. The missions were the main target. The Franciscans would no longer receive government support. Instead, they had to help Mexico by paying taxes to the new government and by providing food, shelter, and clothing to Mexican soldiers stationed in Alta California.

Mexico also planned to strip the Catholic Church of some of its power in Alta California by taking the rich mission lands away from the Franciscans. The Mexican government wanted to make the valuable farmland available to its citizens. Mexico also sought to end the practices of not paying neophytes for their labor and of forcing them to stay at the missions.

Californios (people of Spanish descent who had settled in Alta California) were also eyeing mission property. For years they had been envious of the Franciscans' wealth and free labor force. The land-hungry Californios encouraged the Mexican government to pass laws to redistribute Church holdings.

*"Ever since the independence of Mexico, the missions have been going down; until, at last, a law was passed, stripping them of all their possessions."*

Richard Henry Dana, Jr.
Two Years Before the Mast

## New Laws

In the 1830s, Richard Henry Dana, Jr., a U.S. sailor who traded with the missions, wrote, "Ever since the independence of Mexico, the missions have been going down; until, at last, a law was passed, stripping them of all their possessions."

In 1833 the Mexican government began to pass a series of laws to secularize Alta California's 21 missions. Secularization laws gave the Mexican government the right to take over mission land and property. The churches would remain intact but the missionaries would be replaced by secular priests—priests who performed church services but did not try to convert people to the Catholic faith. In addition, neophytes would be allowed to leave the missions.

Ranchero, *by James Walker, shows the strength and pride of the Alta California rancher.*

The government sent civil administrators to determine the value of each mission and then to divide up land and property among Californios and neophytes. Many of the administrators, however, were corrupt. They took land for themselves or sold it to friends and relatives at low prices. In the end, most ex-neophytes received little or nothing.

## A Taste of Freedom

After many years at the missions, the former neophytes were now on their own, free from the laws of the Church. Some of these Native Americans, who felt they had been slaves to the padres, were overjoyed with their new freedom. But other ex-neophytes did not know what to do or where to go. For years their lives had been controlled by the priests.

During secularization, former neophytes had only a few options. Some longed to return to

# Kitsepawit (Fernando Librado)

Kitsepawit, a Chumash Indian, was born in 1839 in a village called Swaxil, on Santa Cruz Island. Named Fernando Librado by the padres at Mission San Miguel, Kitsepawit lived into the twentieth century. Before his death, Kitsepawit provided U.S. historian John P. Harrington with details about traditional Chumash ways. The Indian also told many stories about the missions and about how the system nearly destroyed Native American culture:

*I once went over to Donociana's house. . . . I wanted to learn the Swordfish Dance. After the meal I asked her to teach me the old dances, saying, "For you are the only ones left who know the old dances." Donociana began to cry, and I left saying nothing more.*

their old lifestyle but had no village to go home to. In some cases, disease had wiped out their communities. In addition, the livestock of the missions had destroyed the region's native grasses—a food source for the native peoples and the animals they hunted. Ex-neophytes who did not have villages to return to either formed small settlements of their own or moved farther inland to join different tribes.

Ex-neophytes who received mission land from the Mexican government tended their fields and tried to earn a living by selling their produce to Californios. But many of these people resented the Indians for owning property and did not want to do business with them. Settlers eventually tricked the Indians, most of whom had never been taught to read, into signing contracts to sell their land at low prices.

Some ex-neophytes who lost their land—or had never received any—went to nearby pueblos or ranchos to live and work. Most ranchers treated Native Americans poorly, paying them little or nothing for long workdays.

Some ex-neophytes stayed at the missions because they had never known any other way of life. These Indians helped the padres farm the land. Many remained until the government sold or gave the mission land away, which usually took years. But with a much smaller workforce than before, the missions declined. Crops lay unharvested in fields, livestock roamed free, and buildings crumbled.

## San Antonio

Secularization at Mission San Antonio de Padua took place in 1834. Padre Juan Cabot, the Spanish-born priest in charge of the mission at the time, was replaced by Padre José Mercado, a Franciscan from Mexico. Padre

# Richard Henry Dana, Jr.

Richard Henry Dana, Jr. (1815–1882), published *Two Years Before the Mast*, a popular sea story, in 1840. Dana, who worked as a sailor between 1834 and 1836, wrote about his adventures while on board a trading ship that sailed from Boston, Massachusetts, to Alta California and back. His work also gives readers an understanding of conditions in Alta California during secularization. About the different classes of people, he wrote:

*The least drop of Spanish blood . . . is sufficient to raise one from the position of a serf, and entitle him to wear a suit of clothes—boots, hat, cloak, spurs, long knife, all complete, though coarse and dirty as may be—and to call himself [Spanish], and to hold property, if he can get any.*

Mercado had a violent temper and often abused the Native Americans. Because of poor treatment, hundreds of ex-neophytes left the mission. By 1839 the mission's Indian population, which had once reached 1,300, was down to 270.

Because the mission was so unsuccessful under Padre Mercado, the Mexican government returned San Antonio to Franciscan missionaries in 1843. Unable to improve the value of the mission, the missionaries abandoned the site the following year. Meanwhile, the governor of Alta California—Pío Pico—tried unsuccessfully to sell San Antonio.

## San Luis Obispo

Padre Martínez had been upset with the secularization laws imposed on the missions by the Mexican government and had many disagreements with Mexican officials. Governor José María Echeandía, the first

*In 1830 Mexican authorities arrested Father Luís Martínez, the priest in charge at Mission San Luis Obispo, for speaking out against secularization*

Mexican governor of Alta California, arrested the outspoken padre and sent him back to Spain in 1830.

Hundreds of neophytes who were loyal to Padre Martínez left the mission in anger. Only about 300 neophytes remained, and many of them were dying from disease.

San Luis Obispo was secularized in 1835. At that time, the

administrator valued the land and animals at $70,000. But after secularization, ranchers and non-mission Indians stole San Luis Obispo's livestock and drove off its horses.

In 1845 Governor Pico sold Mission San Luis Obispo to James Scott, John Wilson, and James McKinley—three pioneers from the United States—for only $510. The men probably hired ex-neophytes to tend the fields and herd the cattle.

## Soledad

Mission Soledad began to crumble even before its secularization in 1835. The aging Padre Sarría, who had come to Soledad in 1828, was the last Franciscan priest stationed at the mission. Shortly after Father Sarría's arrival, the Salinas River flooded again. Later, the mission church collapsed, forcing the padre to use another building for the chapel. Neophytes, aware that they would soon be free, began to leave the mission.

Without a labor force, the mission's buildings could not be repaired. The aqueduct ditches fell out of use. The vineyards weren't tended, and the mission bells stood quiet. Alfred Robinson, an American, noted that Soledad was "the gloomiest, bleakest . . . looking spot in [Alta] California!" Another pas-

Alfred Robinson (1807–1895) was one of dozens of Americans living in Alta California during secularization. He first came to the region in 1829 as a clerk aboard a trading vessel owned by Bryant, Sturgis & Company. Robinson's job was to acquire cow hides and tallow produced by the missions and Californios. In 1846 he published *Life in California,* one of the few books that recounts what it was like to live in Alta California in the 1830s.

serby, Ross J. Browne, reported that "a more desolate place cannot well be imagined."

In 1835, just before Soledad was secularized, Padre Sarría died. Neophytes carried his body 25 miles to Mission San Antonio for burial. Afterward, mission life at Soledad ended. Most of the Indians did not return.

*Neophytes transport the body of Padre Vicente Sarría from Mission Soledad to Mission San Antonio, where the former father-president would be buried.*

Afterward, the Mexican government took the roof tiles off the mission's buildings and sold the tiles to collect Soledad's taxes. The adobe, left unprotected from rain, slowly washed away. In 1846 Governor Pico sold 8,900 acres of the mission's land to Feliciano Soberanes for $800.

## San Miguel

San Miguel was one of the last of the 21 missions in Alta California to be secularized. An administrator came to the site in the summer of 1836. He counted and recorded everything at the mission, which included 13,000 head of livestock

> "MEXICO HAS PASSED THE BOUNDARY OF THE UNITED STATES, HAS INVADED OUR TERRITORY, AND [HAS] SHED AMERICAN BLOOD UPON AMERICAN SOIL."
> PRESIDENT JAMES K. POLK

and 22 acres of vineyards. The administrator placed the total value of the mission at $82,600. San Miguel had been a successful business.

*James K. Polk*

The administrator divided up some of the mission land and property among the ex-neophytes. Rather than stay and farm, many of the Indians chose to return to their villages in the interior. In July 1846, Governor Pico sold what remained of San Miguel to Petronillo Rios and William Reed. Three days after the purchase, U.S. commodore John Sloat sailed into Monterey Bay. On board his flagship, the *Savannah,* were 250 U.S. marines and sailors.

*Pío Pico*

During the Mexican War, San Luis Obispo (above left) was the site of a military takeover. Upon hearing that the mission was occupied by hostile Mexicans, John C. Frémont (above), an ambitious officer of the U.S. Army, stormed the building only to find a peaceful group of women and children.

# U.S. Invasion

For years the United States had been seeking to acquire land belonging to Mexico. In 1845 the two countries began bickering about the correct borderline between Mexico and Texas, a newly acquired U.S. territory. In May 1846, U.S. president James K. Polk declared, "Mexico has passed the boundary of the United States, has invaded our territory, and [has] shed American blood upon American soil." The Mexican War had begun.

News of the war was out when the *Savannah* docked. The marines quickly put up the flag of the United States. The Mexican flag came down. Commodore Sloat claimed for the United States all the seaports between San Diego in the south and San Francisco in the north. Many Californios—who had been unhappy with the unstable Mexican government—did not resist the invasion. Some even had

been hoping for a U.S. takeover. Others fought to defend their homeland against the U.S. forces.

Overall the U.S. military had little trouble with Mexican resistance in Alta California. Mexico could not afford to station an army in Alta California, so militias (small squads of soldier-citizens) defended the region. These Californios were not well trained, and many of them were not loyal to Mexico. Nevertheless, Mexican forces commanded several victories in southern Alta California. In time, however, the United States successfully occupied the entire territory.

In less than two years, the warring nations signed a peace treaty. Under the agreement, Alta California and other Mex-

*From 1846 to 1848, Mexico battled U.S. forces (above). Throughout the war, the U.S. flag flew over Monterey Bay (right) in Alta California.*

ican territories became part of the United States. Shortly afterward, on September 9, 1850, Alta California became known as California—the thirty-first state of the United States.

Meanwhile, gold had been discovered in a stream on the western slopes of the Sierra Nevada, a mountain range in eastern California. The news spread, and before long immigrants were coming to California from all over the world. Some walked or rode in wagons pulled by mules or oxen. Others came on sailing ships.

Although the richest deposits of gold lay about 100 miles north of the inland valleys, thousands of miners were soon searching the region's waterways. Shopkeepers, tradespeople, and farmers came to make money by supplying the miners with goods and food.

These newcomers brought great changes to the lives of Californios and Native Americans.

In search of fertile soil and deposits of gold, the outsiders paid little attention to boundaries. Called squatters, some people simply settled on ranchos, on the land of ex-neophytes, and within the territories of non-mission tribes.

> MEANWHILE, GOLD HAD BEEN DISCOVERED ON THE WESTERN SLOPES OF THE SIERRA NEVADA.

Legal battles soon followed. To settle land disputes, the U.S. government required the Californios to prove ownership by producing land deeds or other legal documents. But the Mexican government had not always provided such documents, and many Californios had a difficult time proving their ownership. As a result, most Californios lost the land they had received during secularization.

Native Americans, on the other hand, did not enjoy equal protection under the laws. Even when Indians did have proof of land ownership, they lost their property because they were not allowed to testify in court. In addition, many former neophytes lost the property given to them during secularization when the U.S. government returned mission buildings to the Catholic Church in the 1850s and 1860s.

By the mid-1800s, the U.S. government had established a number of **reservations** to house the surviving Indians. Although these lands were reserved solely for Indians, the areas usually had poor soil. Unable to grow enough food in the poor soil, the Indians had to rely on food supplies from the U.S. government.

# PART FOUR

# The Missions in Modern Times

SPAIN'S PLAN FOR THE MISSIONS IN ALTA CALIFORNIA had failed. Mexico had lost the territory to the United States. The quadrangles were abandoned, the missionaries and neophytes long gone.

After secularization the missions of Alta California were nearly forgotten. But in 1884, the journalist Helen Hunt Jackson sparked an interest in the mission period that spread statewide. In that year, Jackson's novel *Ramona* appeared in bookshops. The romantic

*In the late 1800s, the British artist Edwin Deakin began to paint the California missions. His works sparked an interest in restoring the decaying buildings. By this time, little remained of Nuestra Señora de la Soledad.*

*The American writer Helen Hunt Jackson desperately tried to convince U.S. legislators in the late 1800s to pass laws that would give Native Americans more rights. When the government did not respond to her pleas, Jackson wrote* Ramona, *a novel designed to let the public know how badly the Indians had been treated. The best-selling novel, however, only encouraged readers to visit the missions and to plan for their renovation.*

story—written to show how poorly Indians had been treated by Americans in California—ended up causing readers to glorify the mission era. People suddenly wanted to visit the mission buildings.

Although the U.S. government had returned mission buildings to the Catholic Church, the Church did not have the funds to maintain them. By the late 1800s, most of the structures were in ruins.

In 1903 California senator Joseph Knowland formed an organization called the California Historic Landmarks League, which collected money for mission restoration. Senator Knowland traveled all over the state talking to citizens about early California history and the beauty of the original mission buildings. The senator wanted to restore the mission buildings as a way to attract visitors to the state.

## San Antonio

Mission San Antonio, the largest mission in northern California, was the league's first choice for restoration. But the job was bigger than people realized. The mission needed many repairs, and the league could not collect enough money for the project.

Pictures of Mission San Antonio taken in 1890 showed several buildings still standing, but doors were gone. Local ranchers had used the mission's roof tiles and door handles and hinges for their own houses. A fence was built around the mission to keep out stray animals.

On June 13, 1903, the feast day of Saint Anthony, a celebration took place in the ruins of the mission church. Indians played drums, violins, and flutes as neophytes had years before. Some of the musicians were descendants of Salinan and Chumash neophytes.

*By the time Helen Hunt Jackson's novel was published in 1884, Mission San Antonio was a shambles.*

In the 1850s, stagecoaches began running along El Camino Reál, transporting people and mail. Jolon, a small town near Mission San Antonio, became a stopover for the coaches. People passing through the valley sometimes stayed in the mission's buildings overnight. During this period, a Mexican Indian priest watched over the mission buildings. But after his death in 1882, the quadrangle quickly fell apart. Nearby ranchers vandalized the buildings, stealing religious objects, door hinges, and metal door handles. Thieves also removed and sold the mission's roof tiles.

The celebration boosted interest in San Antonio's restoration, which started soon after the festival. Horse-drawn wagons hauled sunbaked adobe bricks, roof tiles, and tools to the mission.

But two natural disasters hampered progress. In 1904 and 1905, heavy rains washed away the adobe of some of the restored buildings. In 1906 an earthquake shook the structures and undid months of hard work.

Although the volunteers were determined to finish the project, the California Historic Landmarks League ran out of funds in 1907 and could not afford to complete the quadrangle. Contributors didn't want to give any more money to what they saw as a defeated project. They were convinced that floods or earthquakes would eventually destroy the restored buildings.

The mission church became a local parish in 1928. By that time, even the restored area was in disrepair. Winds and bad weather had ruined the church roof.

Financed by the Hearst Foundation, a second restoration of Mission San Antonio began in 1948. Catholic priests, working with descendants of neophytes, led the effort. The laborers used rounded roof tiles and adobe brick, just as the original builders had done. In addition, the workers added steel and concrete beams to the thick adobe walls to strengthen them. Eventually, all the mission's buildings were completely rebuilt.

In the 1990s, Mission San Antonio looks as it did when the original Spanish padres and neophytes lived there. It is the only Franciscan mission in California whose natural surroundings have not been altered. Many rooms in the mission are open to the public. When visitors stand outside the church, all of the buildings within view belong to the mission. In the distance are the large oak trees that have long been a common sight in the valley.

## San Luis Obispo

In the mid-1800s, migrants from Mexico and from the United States traveled through California along El Camino Reál. Some of them formed a small community, San Luis Obispo, near the mission.

In 1868 the settlers remodeled the mission church. They covered the outsides of the adobe buildings with white panels of wood and replaced the roofs with wooden shingles. They added a belfry and made the old Spanish church look more like the style of churches found in New England. Small businesses soon surrounded the new wooden church. By 1875 a hotel and a market were sharing the street near the mission. Horse-drawn streetcars provided transportation to residents who built houses near the small town.

By 1890 the town of San Luis Obispo had become a large and active settlement where a variety of ethnic groups made their homes. The old mission church served as a courthouse and jail. Many residents of San Luis Obispo did not even know there had been a mission in the town.

*An arbor of grapevines provides a shady walkway at Mission San Luis Obispo de Tolosa.*

69

*Dancers celebrate La Fiesta, a religious festival that originated in Mexico, at Mission San Luis Obispo.*

In 1920 a fire in the church destroyed the wooden roof. Amazingly, the flames did not damage the original ceiling but uncovered designs the neophytes and padres had painted on the beams. Some enthusiastic church members began talking about restoration.

A complete restoration started in 1933. The people of San Luis Obispo wanted the mission church to look as it had when it was first built. They researched the mission's architecture, finding old photos and paintings. Workers removed the white wooden panels from the old church. Soon new adobe walls and clay tiles went up.

Besides the church, only a few other buildings were restored at Mission San Luis Obispo de Tolosa. Businesses located around the mission occupied the space needed to rebuild the entire quadrangle.

The mission still stands in the middle of San Luis Obispo.

Townspeople flock to a plaza in front of the church for traditional celebrations. One of these events is La Fiesta, held every May. The festival begins with the burning of Zozobra, or Old Man Gloom. Participants build a 15-foot-high bonfire, which is supposed to banish all gloomy feelings.

## Soledad

Many of the buildings at Mission Soledad collapsed after a flood in 1832. Part of the chapel that stands on the site was rebuilt by Indians. Other parts of the chapel crumbled after the Mexican government removed the roof tiles.

About 25 years after secularization, the painter Henry Miller visited Mission Soledad. He saw only one building and a small church. Miller described the mission as "a great heap of ruins."

Soledad was the last mission of the chain to be partially re-

stored. A small group of people living three miles from the mission in the little town of Soledad started the project in 1954. They rebuilt the chapel to look much like the original but left untouched the crumbling adobe walls of the other buildings. The church serves as a chapel for the town of Soledad. Open fields, where thousands of livestock once roamed, still surround the mission site.

## San Miguel

After the U.S. government returned Mission San Miguel to the Catholic Church, priests

*Acres of cropland stretch behind the remaining adobe walls (top) of the quadrangle at Mission Soledad. Remodelers added the fountain (bottom) in the courtyard of Mission San Miguel in the twentieth century.*

rented the buildings to various people for about 40 years. The patio in the center of the mission quadrangle housed pigs and cattle. Columns on the old buildings became worn from cattle rubbing against them. Later the patio was used as a corral for horses.

In 1856 Henry Miller reported that Mission San Miguel was "a large square, on which a great number of adobe houses remain, which however, with the exception of the church and a few buildings next to it, are all unroofed." The frescoes showed through the whitewashed walls, but the altar had been stripped of its silver plating.

Over time the mission grounds changed even more. Untended and neglected, the adobe bricks and the clay roof tiles began to crack. The Southern Pacific Railroad removed some neophyte housing to lay train tracks. In 1878 the Catholic Church decided to use San Miguel as a church. Priests came and repaired parts of the structure.

Fifty years later, the Catholic Church returned Mission San Miguel to the Franciscans. Major restoration followed. People from the town of San Miguel and other nearby areas donated money and labor to the project. The people staged *fiestas* (celebrations) to raise the necessary funds.

Workers gently removed the roof tiles and set steel girders under the beams in the ceiling. They replaced some adobe bricks with cement blocks and rebuilt the roof. Copies of the original doors were installed and trees were planted. Volunteers repaired storeroom walls.

The frescoes painted by the neophytes survived. No one painted over them, and no one touched them up.

## Modern Native Americans

During and after the mission period, life for Native Ameri-

> BY 1900 THE NUMBER OF CALIFORNIA INDIANS . . . HAD REACHED AN ALL-TIME LOW OF 15,000.

cans in California changed dramatically. European diseases devastated the native population of the region. By 1900 the number of California Indians—which probably peaked at about 300,000 in the late 1700s—had reached an all-time low of 15,000.

By the 1990s, more than 240,000 Indians (including Native Americans originally from other states) resided in California. About 14 percent of the Indian population lived on reservations. Some groups, including those of the inland valleys, were thought to have died out in the early 1900s. As a result, they are not recognized by the U.S. government and therefore do not qualify for reservation land. To receive government recognition, inland valley Indians are reuniting to revive their languages and traditions.

More than 200 years have passed since Spaniards first traveled El Camino Reál. The missions they built with Native American labor have survived. Many of the Indian people have survived, too, overcoming great hardships and difficulties. The small towns and large cities along the old trail, however, are now home to new life and to different ways.

# AFTERWORD

Each year thousands of tourists and students visit the California missions. Many of these visitors look around and conclude that the missions are the same today as they were long ago. But, over time, the missions have gone through many changes. The earliest structures were replaced by sturdier buildings with tall towers and long arcades. But even these solid buildings eventually fell into ruin and later were reconstructed.

Our understanding of the missions also has changed through the years. Missionaries, visitors, novelists, and scholars have expressed different opinions about the California missions. These observers often have disagreed about the impact of the missions on the Indians in California. And the voices of Native Americans—from the past *and* the present—have continued to shed light on the mission experience.

The early Franciscan missionaries believed that they were improving the local Indians by introducing them to mission life. But visitors from Europe and the United States frequently described the Spanish missions as cruel places. A French explorer in 1786, for example, reported that the priests treated the neophytes like slaves. He was horrified that Spanish soldiers tracked down runaway Indians and whipped them for trying to return to their old way of life.

Many early visitors were truly concerned about the mistreatment of Native Americans. But the foreign travelers, jealous of Spain's hold on Alta California, also criticized the missions as a way to prove that Spain wasn't worthy to possess the region. Similarly, a young man from the eastern United States, visiting Alta California in the 1830s, was saddened to see so much sickness and death at the missions. He advised his fellow Americans that the region would fare much better as a part of the United States.

The missions were all but forgotten during the 25 years following the U.S. takeover of California. The once solid structures decayed into piles of rotting adobe. One U.S. visitor wrote that she doubted if any structure on earth was "colder, barer, uglier, [or] dirtier" than a California mission.

Just when the missions had disappeared almost completely, they came roaring back to public attention. Beginning in the 1880s, dozens of novels and plays about early California described the Franciscan priests as kind-hearted souls who treated neophytes with gentleness and care. This favorable image of the missions became popular because it gave many Californians a positive sense of their own history and identity. The writings also attracted droves of tourists to California. Merchants and business leaders in the state supported the rebuilding of the crumbling missions because it made good business sense.

The missions today are still the subject of a lively debate. Some people continue to believe that the missions brought many benefits to the Indians by "uplifting" them to European ways. But many others, including some descendants of the neophytes, say that the missions destroyed Native American lifeways and killed thousands of Indians. For all of us, the missions continue to stand as reminders of a difficult and painful time in California history.

*Dr. James J. Rawls*
Diablo Valley College

# CHRONOLOGY

*Important Dates in the History of the Missions of the Inland Valleys*

**1769**      San Diego de Alcalá, the first Franciscan mission in Alta California, is founded

**1771**      Franciscans establish Mission San Antonio de Padua

**1772**      Mission San Luis Obispo de Tolosa is founded

**1784**      Father Junípero Serra dies; Father Fermín Francisco de Lasuén becomes the new father-president

**1791**      Father Lasuén sets up Mission Nuestra Señora de la Soledad

**1797**      Mission San Miguel Arcángel is established

**1821**      New Spain gains independence from Spain

**1830s**      Missions are secularized

**1846**      Mexican War begins; U.S. Navy occupies Monterey

**1848**      Mexican War ends; Mexico cedes Alta California to the United States

**1850**      California becomes the thirty-first state

**1850s**      U.S. government begins to return the California missions to the Catholic Church; mission buildings are falling apart

**1890s–present**      Missions are restored

# ACKNOWLEDGMENTS

Photos, maps, and artworks are used courtesy of: Laura Westlund, pp. 1, 13, 19, 30, 36, 40, 42, 46 (bottom); © Frank Balthis, pp. 2–3; Southwest Museum, Los Angeles, CA, pp. 8–9 (photo by Don Meyer, CT.374–646.G136), p. 21 (top left) (photo by Lawrence Reynolds, 10.C.53); North Wind Picture Archives, pp. 10–11, 15, 52–53; Independent Picture Service, pp. 12, 25, 26, 32, 39 (left), 58, 59, 62 (right); © John Elk III, pp. 16–17, 37, 51; © Galyn C. Hammond, p. 16 (inset), 47, 71 (bottom); © Jo-Ann Ordano, p. 18; © Eda Rogers, pp. 20, 21 (bottom), 45; © Sherry Shahan, p. 21 (top right); Bancroft Library, pp. 22, 24, 55, 61 (right); © Carol Stiver, pp. 27, 33 (bottom); © Diana Petersen, pp. 28–29, 31, 34 (right), 39 (right); ©Reno A. DiTullio, pp. 33 (top), 71 (top), 72; © Chuck Place, pp. 34 (left), 61 (left); © Richard R. Hansen, pp. 35 (left and bottom right), 70; © Shirley Jordan, pp. 35 (top), 44 (right), 49 (left), 69; © Lynda Richards, pp. 41, 46 (top); Dept. of Library Services, American Museum of Natural History (neg. #4051), p. 43; © Yamada-Lapides Photography, p. 44 (left); John Erste, p. 48; © Peter S. Ford, p. 49 (right); © D. J. Lambrecht, p. 50; Santa Barbara Museum of Natural History, p. 56; Library of Congress, pp. 57 (#LCUSZ62–17981), 62 (left), 66; Huntington Library, p. 60 (left); Architect of the Capitol, p. 60 (right); History Collections, Los Angeles County Museum of Natural History, pp. 64–65; California Historical Society, Title Insurance & Trust Photo Collection, Dept. of Special Collections, Univ. of Southern California Library, p. 67 (neg. #7719); Independent Picture Service, Nancy Smedstad, pp. 74–75; Pauline Brower, p. 80 (top); Dr. James J. Rawls, p. 80 (middle); Prof. Edward D. Castillo, p. 80 (bottom). Cover: (Front) ©Diana Petersen; (Back) Laura Westlund.

Quotations are from the original or translated writings or statements of Juan Quintana, p. 23; Gaspar de Portolá, p. 26; Father Junípero Serra, p. 30; Father Francisco Palóu, pp. 31–32; Father Juan Crespí, p. 40; Father Fermín de Lasuén, p. 47; Father Antonio de la Concepcion Horra, p. 48; Alfred Robinson, pp. 51, 59; Richard Henry Dana, Jr., p. 54; Ross J. Browne, p. 59; James K. Polk, pp. 60, 61; Henry Miller, pp. 70, 72.

| METRIC CONVERSION CHART | | |
| --- | --- | --- |
| **WHEN YOU KNOW** | **MULTIPLY BY** | **TO FIND** |
| inches | 2.54 | centimeters |
| feet | 0.3048 | meters |
| miles | 1.609 | kilometers |
| square feet | 0.0929 | square meters |
| acres | 0.4047 | hectares |
| ounces | 28.3495 | grams |
| pounds | 0.454 | kilograms |
| gallons | 3.7854 | liters |

# INDEX

# ABOUT THE AUTHOR

**Pauline Brower,** a native of California, has written several history books for children, including *Pilgrims Plantation, Algonquian Indians, Canal Boats West, Lighthouse Family,* and *Baden-Powell: Founder of the Boy Scouts.* Her other writing credits include history articles in *Northern Virginia.* Ms. Bower has also produced a series of television shows and conducted workshops in elementary schools on living history and writing. She is a member of the American Historical Society and of the Society of Children's Book Writers and Illustrators. Ms. Brower resides in Corona del Mar, California, with her husband. She has four daughters and five grandsons.

# ABOUT THE CONSULTANTS

**James J. Rawls** is one of the most widely published and respected historians in the field of California history. Since 1975 he has been teaching California history at Diablo Valley College. Among his publications are *Indians of California: The Changing Image, New Directions in California History,* and, with Walton Bean, *California: An Interpretive History.* Dr. Rawls is also the author of several works for young readers, including *Never Turn Back: Father Serra's Mission* and *California Dreaming.* Dr. Rawls frequently serves as a consultant for books, for television and radio programs, and for film documentaries on subjects dealing with California's history.

**Edward D. Castillo** is a direct descendant of Cahuilla-Luiseño Indians who lived at Missions San Gabriel and San Luis Rey. A professor of California Indian ethnohistory for more than 20 years, Castillo offers Native perspectives of mission life to students of California history. His first book is entitled *Native American Perspectives on the Hispanic Colonization of Alta California.* He recently cowrote, with historian Robert Jackson, *Indians, Franciscans and Spanish Colonization: The Impact of the Mission System on California Indians.* Professor Castillo is a founding member of the Native American Studies Departments at the Los Angeles and Berkeley campuses of the University of California. At Sonoma State University, he serves as an associate professor and chairs its Native American Studies Department.